The Bully That Couldn't

Copyright© 2020 Shontel Murrell

No part of this publication may be reproduced, stored, or transmitted in any form or by any means, electronic, mechanical, photocopying, recording, scanning, or otherwise, without the prior written permission of the author, except as permitted under Section 107 or 108 of the 1976 United States Copyright Act.

Requests to the author or publisher for permission should be addressed to Authorshontelm@gmail.com.

Limit of liability/disclaimer of warranty:

While the publisher and author have employed their best efforts in preparing this guide, they make no representation or warranties with respect to the accuracy or completeness of the contents of this document and specifically disclaim any implied warranties of merchantability or fitness for a particular purpose. No warranty may be created or extended by sales representatives, promoters, or written sales materials.

The advice and strategies contained herein may not be suitable for your situation. You should consult with a professional where appropriate. Neither the publisher nor the author shall be liable for any loss of profit or any other commercial damages, including but not limited to special, incidental, consequential, or other damages.

Acknowledgments

Thanks be to God first for my survival from being bullied for simply being me. I survived to tell the story, and I am thankful for my wonderful children and husband, who listened and inspired me to put this book in the hands of a child that would one day need it. My children were the first partakers of this awesome book.

Big thanks to my illustrator and my team that helped bring my inspiring story to life.

Introduction

Journey through the life of a beautiful and intelligent young lady who has a great home life but has issues with school. I wrote this book with the thoughts of my own childhood in mind and how hard it is being a kid growing up while not being accepted by peers.

I wanted to shed light on the importance of knowing who you are to God, first, so that children will be ready at a young age to still be confident in who they were when they came across a bully along the way. You don't have to take insults personally. What you believe about you means more than what anyone else thinks of you.

Affirming children at home is so important because though life may happen, self-confidence cannot be taken away from you. YOU OWN IT!

THE BULLY THAT COULDN'T

Giselle woke up that morning feeling like she did not want to go to school. She was not sure why she felt that way but knew she would have to go to school anyway. She rolled out of bed rather sadly and went into the bathroom to take a bath.

A little while later, she got out of the bathroom, humming her favorite hymn cheerfully, then she saw her school clothes draped over the back of the chair, and she became sad. Giselle now remembered why she was not looking forward to going to school. She picked up the clothes; the dress was green and covered in large blue flowers, and as she placed the blue scarf over her brown hair, she looked at herself in the mirror.

Now, Giselle was a beautiful little girl, but she did not know that. Her green eyes and brown hair were such bright colors, and she looked beautiful. But Giselle did not see any of these things.

"I wish I could look a little different," she thought. *"Not so different that I would be someone else, just different enough so that Lacy won't have anything bad to say to me."*

Lacy was a girl in Giselle's class who always found something wrong with how everyone else looked, and she used it to make fun of them. She was very mean and liked to make people cry, and when they did cry, she enjoyed it immensely and pointed it out to everyone in class.

As Giselle stood in front of the mirror that morning, she tried to spot everything that Lacy could make fun of. Soon, she was tired of it and decided to go to school.

As she went downstairs to the kitchen, her mom and dad were sitting at the table, reading the newspaper and eating their breakfast. As soon as they saw her, they put down their papers, and her father looked her over while her mother got her breakfast.

"Aren't you just the loveliest little lady?" her father said as he picked her up and spun her around.

Giselle laughed hysterically as her father swung her around.

"Your breakfast is going to come right back up, Donald," her mother said, putting down some toast on the table for Giselle.

Her father put her down, and they all laughed as Giselle walked dizzily to her chair, like a drunk person. She loved her parents, and they loved her right back. She always loved spending time with them. It was too bad she had to go to school, Giselle thought.

Later on her way out, she picked up her lunchbox and found a note stuck to it. Giselle's mother was always leaving her little notes. She called them God's reminders.

The one on her lunchbox read,

> "You are so beautiful, and there is nothing wrong with you." – Song of Solomon 4:7.

Giselle wondered if the note could be right. Was it possible that there was nothing wrong with her? Well, God had said it, and God never lies, so it must be right. Giselle cheered up and ran out to meet the school bus, feeling quite merry.

Her happiness did not last for long.

As soon as she stepped off the bus and into school, Giselle's day began to look bad again.

Lacy was standing in the middle of the walkway, talking to Clara and Cathy, her minions. Clara and Cathy followed Lacy everywhere, and they laughed at people when Lacy was

mean to them. Sometimes, Lacy even made fun of them, yet they still hung around her all the time.

Giselle stood for a moment, trying to figure out how she could get past the three girls. She decided to take the walkway at the other end of the school grounds. It meant that she had to walk all the way around to get to her class, but she knew that she would rather walk around the school a dozen times than face Lacy on the walkway.

Giselle took the long walk around the school field and over the playground. She was hot from all the walking she had done when she got to her class, but she was glad that she did not have to meet Lacy.

"Hey, Animalia. Hey, Animal, move!" she heard Lacy call out from behind her. She had been standing at the door to her class, trying to catch her breath.

Giselle turned around to find Lacy glaring at her.

"Why is she an animal, Lacy?" Cathy asked.

"Oh, yes! Why, Lacy?" Clara asked too.

"Because she is named after an animal. Why are you both so stupid?" Lacy said, sounding frustrated.

Giselle tried to quietly sneak to her seat in front of the class while Lacy was yelling at her friends, hoping that she would

not be noticed, but Lacy quickly turned around and faced her again.

"Why are you named after an animal anyway?"

Giselle said nothing.

"Do you think it's because of the nest on your head that makes you look like a scarecrow's best friend?" Clara and Cathy laughed aloud, and Giselle could hear some other people in the class laughing too. She felt as if there was a huge lump in her throat, and there was a stinging feeling in her eyes as tears began to well up.

Giselle walked to her seat, blinking extremely fast to stop from crying.

Lacy and her friends walked to their seats, still laughing.

Giselle's hands were shaking as she sat quietly, trying awfully hard not to cry. No one in the class wanted to say anything to her because they knew it would only make Lacy find something about them to laugh at too.

At that moment, Giselle really hated her name. She wondered why her parents stuck her with a name that was also the name of an animal.

As if everything that had happened to Giselle was not enough, she soon felt a tug at her head, and she felt her scarf being pulled away from her head. She turned around to see

Lacy holding her scarf, and she asked, "Oh, is this yours, flower girl? I thought it was the rag for cleaning the desks." She began to clean a desk with the scarf, as her friends and other classmates laughed.

Giselle could not hold back anymore. She jumped out of her seat, snatched the scarf out of Lacy's hands, and ran away to the bathroom with tears pouring down and her hair tumbling down her face.

In the bathroom, Giselle sat on a toilet seat and cried and cried. She felt so hurt. Why was Lacy always picking on her? She wondered. She had never done anything wrong to Lacy, no one in the class ever had, yet Lacy was always attacking them with words and making them feel bad.

Giselle knew that bullying was wrong, but why didn't Lacy know it?

Was it really terrible that she wore clothes with flowers on them, or that she wore a scarf?

She remembered a verse from the Bible that had been read at Sunday school just the day before.

She remembered clearly; she was the one who had read it out loud to everyone else.

"God judges persons differently than humans do. Men and women look at the face; God looks into the heart." – 1st Samuel 16:17.

She thought to herself, *"God, if you don't look at my hair or face, couldn't you just tell Lacy not to look at them, either?"* She felt bad.

After a few minutes, Giselle got up, washed her face, and walked back to her class, praying silently in her heart that Mrs. Peter, her class teacher, would have been delayed on

her way to class. As she got to the door of her classroom, she could see Mrs. Peter standing in the middle of the class, and her heart sank. She knew she was in trouble, but she did not have a choice, so she walked into the class with her head down.

"Giselle, where have you been? You were marked absent during roll call." Mrs. Peter said.

"I was...I...I was in the ba-ba-bathroom, ma'am." Giselle stuttered.

Someone giggled in the class, and Giselle looked up to see Lacy making faces at her behind Mrs. Peter.

"You were gone for half an hour, Giselle. Did something happen?" Mrs. Peter asked.

Lacy gave Giselle a cold look, daring her to tell Mrs. Peter what had happened in the class before she left. Giselle shook her head, and Mrs. Peter looked at her suspiciously.

"Well, you'd really want to watch what you eat, Giselle, so you don't spend any more class mornings in the bathroom," Mrs. Peter said kindly. "Go take a seat."

Lacy and her friends were giggling in their seats. Giselle wanted to run away, far from school, back to her house, where no one made fun of her.

After school that day, Giselle ran all the way to the school bus and sat in the seat at the farthest back of the bus. It was where all the noisemakers sat, but she did not care. She knew that Lacy would not sit at the back of the bus. Giselle was sad, and she kept stopping herself from crying.

As Giselle got home, she felt much better. She knew that no one would make her cry at home. She also knew that her mother would have made some of her delicious fruity smoothies, and that made her walk faster down the driveway to her house.

As soon as Giselle got in the door, she could smell cake baking in the oven, and she immediately forgot all about school. "Mummy! I'm home!" she shouted, walking into the kitchen where she was certain her mother would be.

Her mother smiled when she saw her, and Giselle skipped towards her for a big warm hug.

"Welcome home, darling. How was school today?" her mother asked.

"School was fine," she said, faking a smile. It was a lie, but she did not want to tell her mother about Lacy. Her mother smiled back at her, patted her head, and then she noticed that Giselle was not wearing her scarf.

"Where is your scarf, Giselle?" her mother asked. Giselle was confused for a while. Then, she remembered she had left it in the bathroom before she returned to class.

"I forgot it at school." She answered, not looking her mother in the face.

"You don't forget things, Giselle. Why did you take it off?" her mother asked further.

Giselle started blinking, tears were gathering in her eyes, and she could not stop them. As she opened her mouth to speak, tears began to roll down her cheeks. Her mother wondered what the problem could be. She patted Giselle's shoulder and dabbed at her face with the ends of her apron.

"Mummy, there is a girl called Lacy in my class," Giselle said, but then she stopped. She was not sure if she should tell her mother. Wouldn't that make her a baby? She looked up to see her mother looking at her, waiting for her to answer.

Giselle could not help it anymore, and she told her mom everything; about how Lacy always called her ugly, how she sometimes spilled ink on her books, and how she told everyone to call Giselle "animal" because of her name.

After listening to Giselle's tearful story, her mother hugged her tightly, wiped her eyes, and told Giselle to go to her room to wash up and come back down for cake and smoothies. She did not say a word about what

Giselle had told her.

As Giselle walked up the stairs, she wondered what it meant. Did her mother think she was being a baby? Was she truly angry at Lacy? Giselle wondered what her mother was thinking.

Maybe her mother did not really understand what it all meant. Maybe she did not think the whole thing was serious. Giselle stood in front of the mirror after her bath. She poked at her cheeks and peered into her eyes. She could not see anything that should make her think she was ugly.

Why did Lacy just keep saying that she was? Maybe she was ugly, but maybe she could not see the ugliness because it was her own face.

She heard her father drive into the garage, and she quickly dashed out of her room and began to run down the stairs.

As she walked into the kitchen, her father, who was already seated at the table, began to shout into a rolled up piece of paper, "Here is an incredibly beautiful girl coming through. Make way. Make way. Make way for the most beautiful girl in the entire universe."

Giselle chuckled and ran to give him a hug. *"Silly Daddy!"* she thought. He probably could not see that she was ugly because he was her father, and he loved her so much.

As they ate delicious cake and drank their smoothies, Giselle's mother asked her to tell her father the story about Lacy and her bullying. Giselle was reluctant to talk about what had happened, but she was no longer feeling terrible, so she told her father the whole story without crying.

When she was done telling her story, she asked her parents, "Do you really think I'm pretty? Or are you just saying that because you're my mom and dad?"

Her father chuckled, and her mother smiled.

"Sweetheart," her mother said, "get the Bible from the shelf."

Giselle got up and did as she was told, but she wondered what the Bible had to do with the question she had just asked.

"Read Psalm 139, the fourteenth verse," Giselle's father said.

"I praise you because I am fearfully and wonderfully made. Your works are wonderful. I know that full well," Giselle read.

Giselle felt uncomfortable in her chair; she knew what was coming.

"Do you believe what you just read?" her mother asked.

"Yes, Mom." She answered.

"Well, this should tell you two things," her mother said. "First, you are wonderfully made by God. There is nothing about you that is less than wonderful. Second, when anyone tells you that you are less than wonderful, it is not because of anything that is wrong with you, it is because something is wrong with them."

Giselle sat up in her seat. She had not thought about that. So, Lacy was always making fun of her classmates, not because there was something wrong with all of them, but because something was wrong with Lacy.

"Did you report this matter to any of your teachers?" Her father asked.

"Erm…no, but, well, I don't know." She did not really know what to say.

"Giselle, you have had an anti-bullying rally at your school. Were you not taught to report such things to a teacher?"

"I was taught to do that, Mom, but I didn't say anything because I don't want everybody to think I was a baby," Giselle said.

"Well, your mother and I will go to school with you tomorrow. I would like to have a few words with your Principal about this Lacy girl." Her father said.

Giselle felt happy that her parents cared for her so much, but she also felt bad because she did not want anyone to get into trouble because of her. She thought about what would happen to her after Lacy was punished. "Oh, no!" she thought. It would only get worse. Lacy would pick on her more, and everyone would call her a tattletale.

"Mom, Dad, please don't go to my school tomorrow. I will do anything. I will go to a different school. I could be homeschooled. Please, oh please, do not go to see the Principal.

"Dad, I will wash your car for a year. Please, Mom, don't get Lacy in trouble." Giselle went on and on, pleading and making promises. Her father looked at her, quite amused, while her mother just shook her head and wiped the kitchen table.

"We're going, Giselle," her mother said. "And the main reason we're going is because Lacy needs to understand what she is doing and how wrong it is. If she is not told and punished for what she has done, she will not stop. Do you want all your other classmates to continue suffering as you have been because of Lacy?"

Giselle shook her head no. She really wanted Lacy to stop bullying people; she just wished she did not have to be part of it.

"People who commit offenses need to be punished, so they will know that their actions have consequences." Her father said.

Giselle nodded, but she still wished she did not have to be involved in teaching Lacy a lesson.

All night, she thought about what would happen, and she knew she was doomed.

NEXT DAY

On Tuesday morning, Giselle got up earlier than usual and said a quick prayer, telling God to change her parents' mind about going to school with her.

Two hours later, despite her prayer, she was standing in the hallway, and her mother was saying, "Head to your class, we'll just see the Principal and get going in a few minutes."

Resigned to her fate, Giselle walked to her class. She could not concentrate on her English lesson, and because she was not paying attention, she told Mrs. Peter that the past tense of "bite" was *bited*.

The laughter that followed her answer only caused her more discomfort.

When the Principal's secretary walked into the class and instructed Giselle and Lacy to follow her to the Principal's office, Giselle wanted to leap out of the class through the window. She wanted to run all the way home and crawl under her blanket, but she could not do that, so she followed the Principal's secretary out of the class with Lacy behind her. As they walked down the hallway, there was silence. Because of the Principal's secretary, Lacy did not say anything to Giselle, but she kept giving her terrible looks.

In the Principal's office, Giselle was made to narrate her ordeal with Lacy to the Principal and the Principal's assistant. She stuttered through the whole narration and wished the ground would just open and she would fall inside.

"Lacy, we called your mother, and she said she is really busy at work and cannot come over. What do you have to say for yourself?" The Principal asked.

Lacy stared at her shoes and refused to look up. She was thinking about how she would deal with Giselle, the telltale.

Then, Giselle's mother arrived and was asked to speak. She began to speak, and she said, "Lacy, I don't know the reason you bully people, but I just want to know; If someone else was mean to you and always made you feel bad, how would you feel?"

Lacy refused to lift her head. She had planned that she would not say a word to anyone in the Principal's office, and they might as well just punish her, but the soft tone of Giselle's mother's voice was making her feel uncomfortable.

Giselle's mother continued, "I know a verse in the Bible; Matthew Chapter 7, verse 12. It tells us that we should treat people exactly how we want people to treat us. If you would like for people to treat you nicely and make you feel good, then you should also make people feel good. When you make other people feel good, you will find that you will also begin to feel good."

Lacy had heard that verse in the Bible, but she had never heard it said like that.

"My mother said I am a nuisance," she said. "I heard her talking on the phone to someone at work, and she said, 'I'm trying to get it done, but Lacy is a bit of a nuisance.'" Her eyes glistened with tears as she spoke, and she wondered why she was talking to Giselle's mother about that.

"How did that make you feel, Lacy?" Giselle's mother asked.

Lacy began to cry.

Giselle's mother told her that even if she felt badly hurt, it was very wrong to make other people feel hurt too. She also told her that if she could treat people well, she would feel good.

All through the conversation, Giselle stood in a corner of the office, watching everything that was happening. She had never imagined that it could turn out like that.

Her mom had been right. Lacy was not mean to others because there was something wrong with them; she was

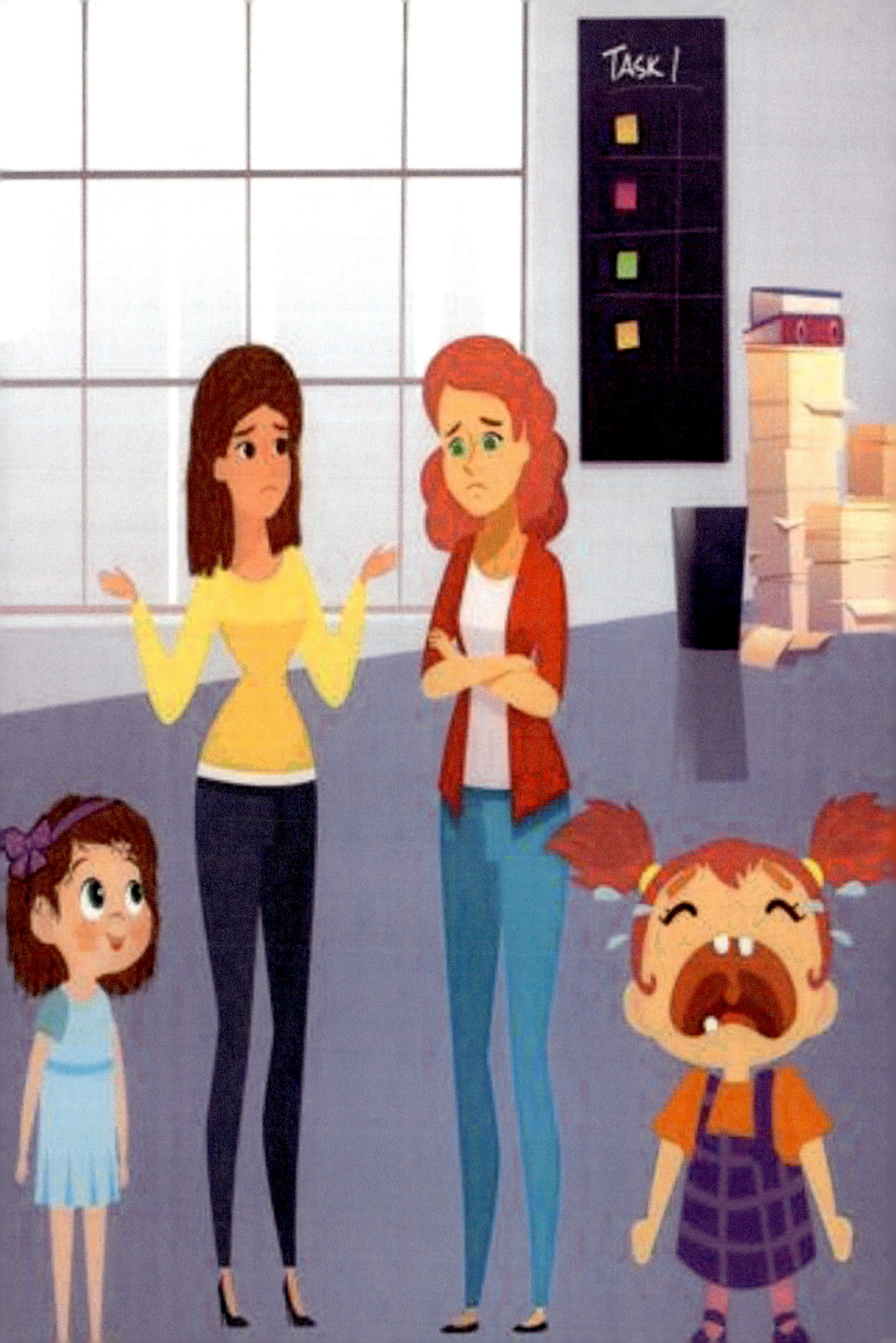
TASK 1

mean because there was something wrong with her. Lacy was given a week in detention for her behavior, and this was the consequence of her actions. Her mom was invited to another meeting with Lacy and Giselle's present as well.

The Principal spoke with Lacy's mom, and said, "Tonya, can you please describe what life is like at home that would cause Lacy to treat others unkind?"

Lacy's mom answered, "It has been so hard, working long shifts, and I do not get to listen to Lacy as I should. I am so sorry this has happened. I give her TV time, and she gets most of the things she wants."

The Principal then spoke, "What seems to be missing at home is attention and love, and Lacy would not take her anger out on other children. We will not tolerate bullying at school. I will offer counseling to Lacy here, and I would like to give you some referrals for family counseling as needed. Every child needs love and attention, as well as a support system, and if you are working long hours and cannot attend to Lacy as you want, she needs an outlet and people that she can trust."

Lacy looked over at her mom, and her mom told her that she was sorry, and Lacy began to weep. Lacy said, "I really like Giselle's clothes, and I wish we could be friends."

Lacy really did like Giselle deep down inside, but she became jealous because she did not get the attention at home.

"Giselle, I am so sorry for hurting you. Will you please accept my apology?" Lacy said.

"Yes, I accept your apology."

The principle interrupted, "Giselle, it is not okay to allow others to mistreat you or others. All adults here have an obligation to report bullying. We want parents to feel comfortable sending their children to school. We do not want anything to stop you from learning and enjoying school and all it has to offer. So, please understand that it is safe to report bullying to an adult so that we can deal with it."

"Okay, I will not hesitate next time."

"Now, I will be in my office typing up behavior notes to notify the parents of the other kids that were involved, so that they too will be held accountable. You all can feel free to talk, or if you would like to go home, that is fine. I believe we have taken care of the problem," said the Principal.

"I would like to give you my contact info, Tonya, and I would like to invite you and Lacy to lunch and Bible study with us one day, if that is okay with you. It takes a village to teach and mold our kids in the correct way," Giselle's mom said. "I am up for it, sounds great," said Lacy's mom.

At last, the bullying issue was solved, and the bully was stopped in her tracks. Everyone in the meeting shook hands and went on to enjoy the rest of the beautiful summer day.

THE END.

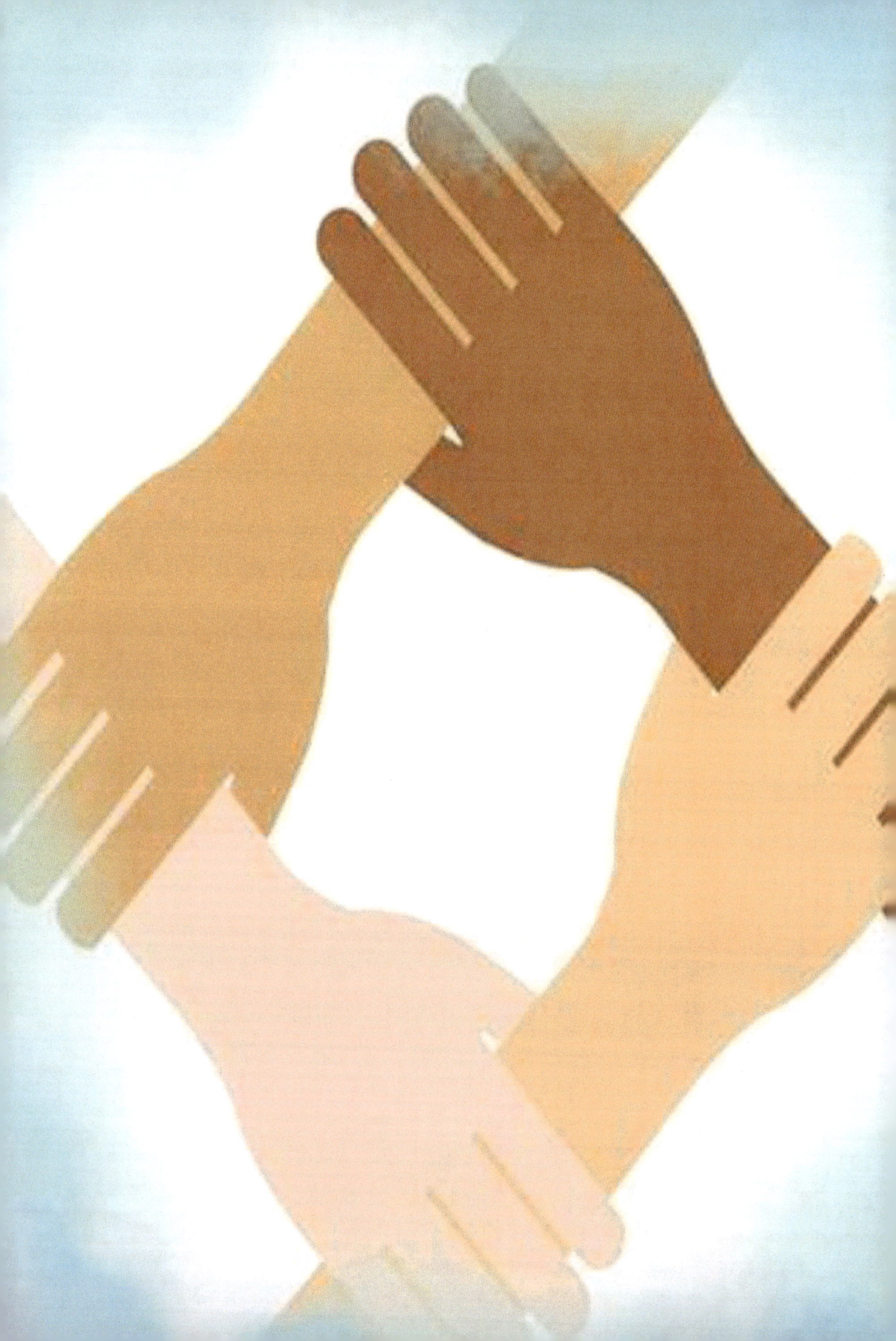

Part 1: Q&A

Q1: What did you learn about bullies?

Q2: Why do bullies bully?

Part 2

Pick the Best answer and circle it.

Q3: How would you deal with a bully?
A: Hit them.
B: Tell an adult on them.
C: Run away from them.

Part 3

Read the question below and write a sentence to describe your answer.

Q4: How do you stop the cycle of bullying?

True or False Questions:

1. God thinks that you are not good.
2. God thinks you are beautiful and amazing.
3. God looks at the clothes you have on.
4. God looks at the heart.

Answer Key:

1. False
2. True
3. False
4. True

Reflection of Story

Directions: Use this page to discuss what you learned while reading this book.

Made in the USA
Columbia, SC
01 October 2021